In the Middle Ages farmers reared sheep for wool & for meat

Scotland

Ireland

King's Lynn

Bristol

London

English ships carried wool to Europe

France

OXFORD
UNIVERSITY PRESS

Great Clarendon Street, Oxford OX2 6DP

Oxford University Press is a department of the University of Oxford.
It furthers the University's objective of excellence in research, scholarship,
and education by publishing worldwide in

Oxford   New York

Auckland   Cape Town   Dar es Salaam   Hong Kong   Karachi
Kuala Lumpur   Madrid   Melbourne   Mexico City   Nairobi
New Delhi   Shanghai   Taipei   Toronto

With offices in

Argentina   Austria   Brazil   Chile   Czech Republic   France   Greece
Guatemala   Hungary   Italy   Japan   Poland   Portugal   Singapore
South Korea   Switzerland   Thailand   Turkey   Ukraine   Vietnam

Oxford is a registered trade mark of Oxford University Press
in the UK and in certain other countries

First published 1945

This edition 2007

British Library Cataloguing in Publication Data

Data available

ISBN-13: 978-0-19-911571-6

3 5 7 9 10 8 6 4 2

Printed in Singapore by Imago

Every care has been taken to trace copyright. In the event of any error, we apologise and will,
if informed, endeavour to make corrections in any future editions.

DRAWN DIRECT TO THE PLATE BY CLARKE HUTTON AND LITHOGRAPHED IN GREAT BRITAIN BY
W. S. COWELL, LTD., IPSWICH.

A
PICTURE HISTORY
OF
BRITAIN

CLARKE HUTTON

OXFORD
UNIVERSITY PRESS

Clarke Hutton
(1898–1984)

Clarke Hutton studied at the Central School of Arts & Crafts in London from 1927–1930 and was taught lithography by A.S. Hartrick, one of the foremost lithographers of his day. On Hartrick's retirement, Clarke Hutton took over his teaching at the School and remained there from 1930–1968.

During this period he became a very well known and respected lithographer. Working largely in this medium he became a successful book illustrator working for a range of publishers including Oxford University Press, Penguin, Dent, The Folio Society and NY Limited Editions Club.

Through his Central School connections he was one of the first artists to use the 'autolithographic technique' for his book illustrations and was part of designer Noel Carrington's team of artists who produced the inexpensive, attractive and innovative Picture Puffins series, along with Pearl Binder, Kathleen Hale and several other Central School artists. He used the same technique for the set of extraordinary, educational prints he produced for Oxford University Press in the 1950s which informatively decorated the walls of many school classrooms of that time.

Like many artists of the period who taught at the Central School, his major contribution can be seen as the passing on of skills and traditions to the next generation, especially illustrators. His students included Peggy Fortnum, Judith Kerr, Susan Einzig, John Burningham and Faith Jaques.

His work forms part of the valuable educational resource of the Central Saint Martins Museum, Archive and Study Collection and is a source of inspiration to new generations of artists, designers and illustrators.

The republishing of this delightful book demonstrates the qualities and role that high quality illustration and visual interpretation still play in stimulating thinking. It might even inspire students to find ways to visually express themselves and the world they live in, through this vibrant and highly personal form of expression, so well presented here by one of Britain's most skilled and inspiring illustrators of the twentieth century.

Chris Wainwright
Dean of Art
Central Saint Martins College of Art and Design

EARLY BRITAIN

Before there was any written history in Britain men and women lived in caves surrounded by forests and wild animals, making themselves knives, choppers, spearheads and such things out of stone.

Gradually they began to build huts and live in villages, usually near rivers or lakes. They made tools and weapons from bone. They learnt to make and use fire, and built temples with great blocks of stone. For clothes they wore the skins of animals.

Later "Celtic" people invaded Britain from Europe and settled there. They made bronze and iron ware, built boats, used horses and probably introduced the wheel. They became traders and sailed to and from northern France.

Phoenicians and Greeks from the Mediterranean sailed to Britain to exchange goods. They used money and made coins of iron, silver and tin.

By 55 B.C. the Roman Empire had spread to northern France and from there Julius Caesar invaded the shores of Britain. He was beaten off, but 99 years later the Romans did land on the coast of Kent. Some of the British tribes fought fiercely against them. Boadicea, Queen of the Iceni tribe, was one of the British leaders, but eventually the Romans conquered and ruled Britain for nearly 400 years.

They were good rulers. They made laws for the whole country, kept peace, built cities with fine straight connecting roads, encouraged industries and introduced glass-making.

The Romans were fine builders and engineers. They laid drains and water pipes, had central heating, and built public baths and great outdoor theatres.

Trade increased and London, which had grown up at a spot where the River Thames could be easily crossed, became an important town.

It was surrounded by a high wall in which were several gates, and there is a street in London today called London Wall, where part of the Roman wall can still be seen.

At last the Roman Empire began to weaken. It was being attacked from all sides, and the Emperor in Rome had to call back his soldiers from all over the Empire to defend the homeland.

Britain was then left without an army and at the mercy of the Angles, Saxons and Jutes, who came from Northern Germany. At first they only plundered the country near the coast, carrying off cattle and taking prisoners for slaves, but when they found they could do this quite easily they became bolder and invaded Britain, conquered it and settled down.

ANGLO-SAXON BRITAIN

The language and customs of these invaders were different from those of the Roman-British. They were much more primitive.

In 597 a monk named Augustine was sent to Britain by Pope Gregory. The Pope was head of the Christian Church at Rome. Augustine preached Christianity to the Anglo-Saxons (English), and many of them were converted. The Church was the source of law, justice and learning, and Augustine became the first Archbishop of Canterbury.

Much of the history of this time we learn, from the writings of a monk called the Venerable Bede.

Then the Danes landed on the east coast, and overran the whole of England except the part ruled by Alfred the Great, which was called Wessex and was in the south. Alfred kept them out of Wessex. He reigned for thirty years and did great good for the people. His capital city was Winchester.

Alfred's son was the first king of all England.

The Danes continued to land in England and fight against the English, and for a short time the Danish King Canute reigned, but in 1042 the English Edward the Confessor became King. He founded the first Westminster Abbey. After him came Harold.

The English were great farmers.

The homes of the poor were smoky huts, but those of the well-to-do were made of timber with thatched roofs, consisting usually of one large room or hall. There are a few stone Anglo-Saxon churches still standing in England today, such as St. Peter's at Barton-on-Humber in Lincolnshire.

The next and last invasion of England was made by the Normans, who came from Normandy in northern France. Under their leader Duke William they landed in 1066, fought and won the Battle of Hastings against Harold, who was killed. William the Conqueror became King of England.

NORMAN ENGLAND 1066-1272

William proclaimed that the whole country belonged to him, but he let the Norman nobles, called Barons, have large estates, so long as they fought for him and paid him taxes. In 1085 he had made the famous Domesday Book, in which was described in detail almost every acre of land throughout the country. This enabled William to keep a record of the taxes due to him.

The nobles built themselves great stone castles and often fought each other.

They had followers of knights, squires and soldiers, and when there was no real war they enjoyed mock battles, called tournaments, in the courtyards of their castles.

The Normans and the English soon mixed together, though for some time the King and his Court and the Barons spoke French, while the peasants spoke English.

In the homes of the wealthy were many servants. People were great eaters, their food being mostly salted meats, venison or deer, dried fruits, honey, bread, ale and wine. Sometimes they ate whale.

In 1170 Archbishop Thomas Becket was murdered by some of Henry II's officers because he felt that the rule of the Church

should come before the law of the land. The people looked upon him as a saint and made pilgrimages to the place of his death at Canterbury.

The people were very religious, and monasteries, churches, cathedrals, almshouses and hospitals were built, and many knights and noblemen went with the Crusaders. These were armies of Christian soldiers who travelled across Europe to what is now called Palestine and there made war against the Muslims to recapture the Temple at Jerusalem for the Christians. These adventures were never wholly successful.

In 1199 John became King. He was hated by the Barons and the common people alike, but he is important in English history because at Runnymede on the River Thames the Barons made him seal the Magna Carta. In this document John agreed to give up much of his power and rights to the Barons.

About this time many friars called "Franciscans" travelled over the country and preached the gentle, peace-loving lessons of St. Francis. Wherever they went they were loved and made welcome.

Many new schools were opened, and Latin Grammar was the chief subject taught. The first colleges at Oxford and Cambridge were founded.

Friar Roger Bacon was a scientist. He invented spectacles and gunpowder and planned a telescope.

But in spite of the spread of religion and increase in knowledge of science, many people still believed in magic and witches.

MIDDLE AGES 1272-1485

By now the country was settling down and becoming more united. From time to time Edward I, who came to the throne in 1272, called a meeting of Barons and important men from the counties and big towns to discuss the country's affairs, and, though there had been a King's Council before, this was the real beginning of Parliament. Gradually there came into being two governing houses, the House of Lords, which consisted of the barons, nobles and bishops, and the House of Commons, whose members were chosen from the big towns and shires.

Laws were made and written down, courts were set up, and the King's Judges had to see that the laws were carried out throughout the land.

Edward I conquered Wales and tried, without success, to conquer Scotland. His son was the first Prince of Wales.

Edward III wanted to be King of France as well as King of England, and in order to do this he began the Hundred Years War against France. He was successful at first and won the Battle of Crecy in 1346. The English archers were famous for their skill with the longbow.

In 1349-50 there was a terrible plague called the Black Death. Thousands of people died, so that not enough food was produced and what there was cost more than most people could afford.

As looking after animals employed fewer men than growing wheat, farmers took to sheep-breeding, which was useful both for wool and meat. English ships carried the wool to Europe, particularly to Flanders. Merchants grew rich and built themselves fine houses in the Cotswold Hills, where the sheep grazed, and in East Anglia, from where the ships sailed.

So trade and prosperity increased. Towns grew larger, though the streets were often very narrow and dirty. Most towns were surrounded by walls with gates which were shut at sunset. Each large town was governed by a mayor and council, chosen by the townspeople themselves.

It was usual for tradesmen of the same trade to live and work in the same streets, which were known by the trade name, such as Ironmonger Lane, Haymarket, and others still existing in London and other towns today.

Craftsmen formed themselves into Craft Guilds, such as the Goldsmiths. These Guilds protected their members and saw that they were well treated by their masters and properly paid. They also kept the secrets of their crafts to themselves, and a man could not join a Guild until he was a first-class workman. Seven years were thought necessary to learn some crafts, and while a boy was learning he was called an apprentice.

Many Guilds used to produce each year a religious play, in which they acted such subjects as the Creation of the World or the story of David and Goliath. These were called mystery plays and were acted in the city streets, to the joy of all the townsfolk.

In the open country there were manors. These were estates granted to knights by the king for good service. The Knight was the Lord of the Manor and was the master of all peasants living on his land. They were called serfs and were little better than slaves. In return for their cottages and small strips of land they had to work on the land for him, and he had the right to punish them for small crimes. They were never allowed to go away. If he were a bad master he made them work very hard. The serfs were very unhappy about this. They wanted to be free men, work on their own land and pay rent for their homes. So in 1381, 100,000 peasants followed Wat Tyler to complain to the king. The young Richard II met them and made many promises, but these he was never able to keep.

A famous writer, Geoffrey Chaucer, lived at this time. He wrote the "Canterbury Tales", which are the stories different pilgrims told to each other on their way to Canterbury. They were such good stories that we enjoy them even today.

John Wycliffe first translated the Bible into English in 1380. All his life he tried to reform the Church, which he thought was becoming too rich and unchristian. He was one of the earliest thinkers whose writings and preachings led the way to the "Reformation" of the next century.

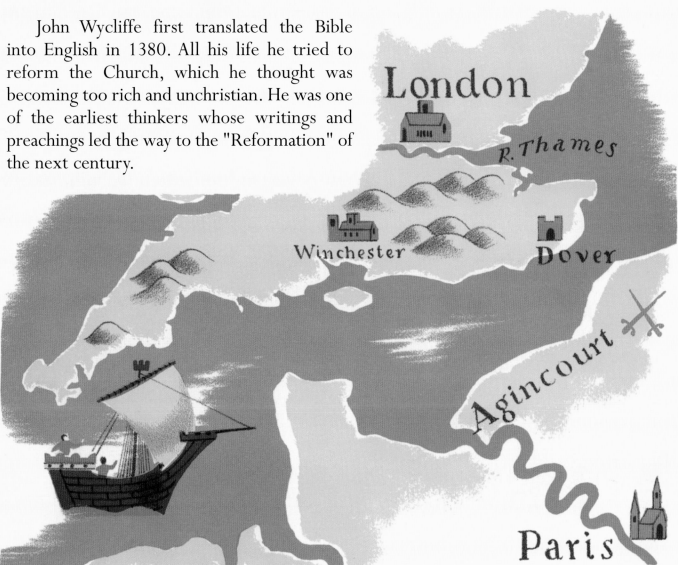

All this time the war with France was going on. Henry V won the battle of Agincourt in 1415; but soon afterwards he died, leaving a baby son as heir to the throne.

Then Joan of Arc appeared and placed herself at the head of the French armies. She said that she was inspired by God, and she put so much heart into the French soldiers that, although she was at last captured and burnt for a witch, the French went on fighting so well that they drove the English out of most of the country they had occupied.

Soon after the soldiers returned to England civil war broke out in 1455 between Henry VI, head of the Lancaster family, and Richard of York, who wanted to be king. The Lancastrians took a red rose and the Yorkists a white one for their badges. These were the Wars of the Roses. The Yorkists won, and Edward, Richard's son, became king. He was a popular and capable ruler.

Architecture had now become delicate, with high arches, towers, and richly coloured windows. This is called the Gothic style, and it is interesting to notice how the people's clothes had the same "frilly" shapes.

In 1476 William Caxton set up the first printing press in England at Westminster in London. Up till this time all books had been handwritten by the monks, who had made it into a very beautiful art, with coloured pictures on many of the pages. The new printing made it possible for more books to be produced and read, so that learning became more general among the people and new schools and colleges were opened.

TUDOR ENGLAND, 1485-1603.

Then followed the period when England became one of the important countries in Europe.

Henry VII encouraged trade and explorers. In 1492 Christopher Columbus, a Genoese sailor, had discovered America, and many other sailors, such as John Cabot, sailed into these new-found oceans seeking fresh lands.

Santa Maria 1492

Henry VIII wanted to rule his own way. At first he took the advice of Cardinal Wolsey, but he quarrelled with him because Henry thought that in England he himself should be head of the Church and not the Pope in Rome. This revolt of Henry's against the Pope was thought to be right by many of the people. It was England's share in the "Reformation" which was going on all over Europe and had been started a century before by John Wycliffe and others.

After Wolsey, Henry made Sir Thomas More his chief adviser. More was a wise man who some time earlier had written a book called "Utopia", in which he had described what he thought was the best way to govern. However, these two quarrelled, and Henry had Sir Thomas More beheaded.

Henry closed all the monasteries in England and took away their lands and money.

He raised England to the position of a first-class power and built a strong navy.

Henry married six times, and had two daughters and one son, Edward VI, who reigned after him for only six years. During this reign a new Prayer Book was written for the reformed Church. Then Mary, Henry's eldest daughter, became queen.

Mary, being a Catholic, married Philip, King of Spain, although this was against the wishes of the English people. During her reign many important people with whom she disagreed were beheaded.

The people became sickened by her cruelties. The more she condemned to death the stronger the hatred grew, and Parliament refused to give way to her on many points. She wanted to undo the Reformation and bring England back to the Roman Church.

Mary died in 1558, and this probably saved the country from a general revolt. The people were filled with joy and hope when Elizabeth came to the throne.

Elizabeth was the second daughter of Henry VIII. She was a clever queen, and during her reign England got back the power and importance it had lost through bad rule in the time of Mary. Elizabeth was a "Protestant", as were the greater number of her subjects, and in her reign the Church of England became the established religion of the people.

The danger to England at that time was Spain. Philip hated England for being Protestant. To weaken the power of Spain Elizabeth encouraged many great sailors, like Drake, Hawkins and Frobisher, to attack Spanish settlements and ships bringing gold home from the New World.

At length in 1588 Philip sent a great fleet called the "Armada" against England, but Lord Howard, Sir Francis Drake and other great sea-captains were on the watch for it. They sank many of the big Spanish ships, and drove the rest up the English Channel as far as Calais, where many more were destroyed by fire.

Sir Francis Drake was the first Englishman to sail right round the world. The voyage, begun in 1577, took nearly three years.

Sea trading was increasing. In 1600 the East India Company was formed and given permission by the Great Mogul, ruler of India, to settle and trade there.

Sir Walter Raleigh sent men to explore the east coast of America. The land they found they called Virginia. There they found tobacco growing and sent some back to England. More and more people began to enjoy smoking a pipe.

A good reform of Elizabeth's was the setting up of the Poor Law. This meant that money and help would be given to those who had no work to do. Before this people out of work had often starved.

Mary, Queen of Scots, was a trouble to Elizabeth.

Although she was the daughter of a Scottish king, she had spent most of her life in France and had married the French king's son. After her husband had died she returned to Scotland to be its queen. She had two more husbands. Her French habits upset the Scottish noblemen, and she had to give up her throne and fly to Elizabeth for help.

But Mary was a Catholic, and Elizabeth suspected her of plotting not only to bring the Catholics back into power, but also, with the help of Spain, to make herself Queen of England. So Elizabeth put her in prison for many years and at last had her beheaded.

This was a time of great poetry, learning and music. Three poets of the day were Shakespeare, Spenser and Ben Jonson. Shakespeare wrote plays which we still enjoy, two famous ones being "A Midsummer Night's Dream" and "Romeo and Juliet." These plays were acted at the Globe Theatre, Southwark, which was then a country place, across the river from London. Today it is one of the busiest parts of the city.

Many big country houses were built by the rich nobles. Inside they were more comfortable than houses built in earlier times. People slept in big four poster beds, and glass instead of horn was put in many windows.

Country dances round the maypole were very popular, being held on village greens and enjoyed by all young people.

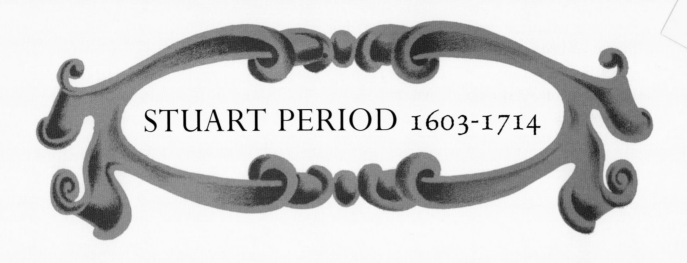

STUART PERIOD 1603-1714

As Elizabeth had no children, James, King of Scotland was next in succession to the throne, and he became king in 1603. He was the first of the Stuart line. He was a Protestant, and during his reign a fresh translation of the Bible was made and this is the version many people read today.

In 1620 a party of English settlers set sail for America in the famous ship "Mayflower" in order that they might be free to worship in their own simple way. They were the "Pilgrim Fathers". Many other people who did not approve of the services of the Church of England were put in prison; they were called "Dissenters".

Charles I became king in 1625. He tried to rule without Parliament, as he believed he could do no wrong and claimed the "Divine right of Kings". He set up law courts of his own where the judges obeyed his wishes.

Charles made war against the Scots. For this he needed money and had to call Parliament and ask for it. Parliament refused. There was civil war. The king's followers were called Cavaliers and those for Parliament, under their leader Oliver Cromwell, were called Roundheads, because they cut their hair short, while the Cavaliers wore theirs long and curly. Cromwell's specially trained soldiers were the "Ironsides".

After many terrible battles the Parliament won. Charles was beheaded and Cromwell became the Protector or Dictator of England.

When Cromwell died the people welcomed Charles II to the throne. Cromwell had been a stern man. Charles was gay and fond of pleasure, and the people longed for a change.

Charles enjoyed the theatre, and a popular actress, Nell Gwynn, who played at Drury Lane Theatre, was a great friend of his.

John Bunyan, one of the "Dissenters", was imprisoned in Bedford Gaol, because he preached so much against the many evils of the times – and while there wrote his famous book "The Pilgrim's Progress."

In 1665 there was a terrible Plague in London, a disease which killed thousands of people. The following year the Great Fire of London broke out, and as most of the buildings were of wood, a great part of the city was destroyed.

Christopher Wren made plans for the rebuilding of London, but he could not carry them out, as the owners of the old houses insisted on rebuilding on the old sites. So Wren could not widen the narrow streets with beautiful broad avenues as he wished, but he rebuilt many of the churches, the most important being St. Paul's Cathedral at the top of Ludgate Hill.

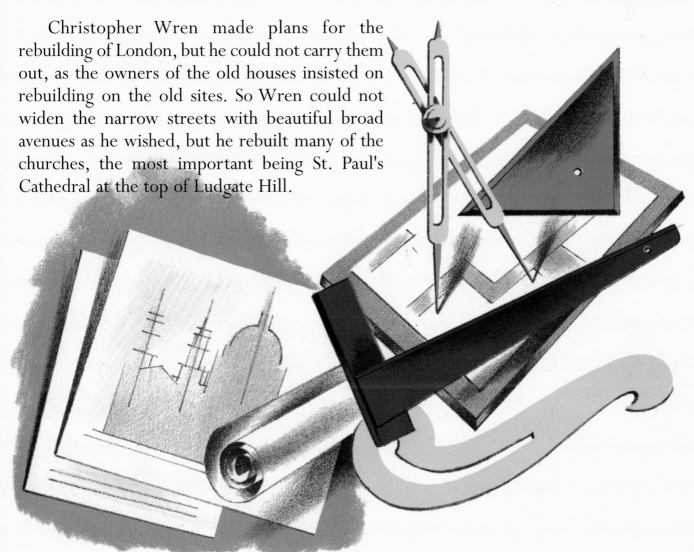

At this time England was at war with Holland for the mastery of the seas. Samuel Pepys, Secretary to the Navy, wrote his famous Diary, telling all that he did from day to day.

James II, a Catholic king, was, like Charles I, unpopular because he wanted to rule without consulting the people through Parliament. There was such an outcry against him that he fled to France in 1688, and the people invited William of Orange, a Dutch Prince, to the throne of England. William was married to Mary, a daughter of James II, and so William and Mary became king and queen. This was called the Glorious Revolution, because no blood was shed.

In 1689 a law was made saying that in future kings must obey the wishes of Parliament, and this law has been kept by English rulers ever since.

William was a better king than England had had for a long time. Under him the navy grew, overseas trade increased, and more people went over to North America, and the colonies there grew in size and number.

During the reign of Queen Anne in the early 1700's, France tried to dominate Europe. There was war, most of the fighting being in the Low Countries, as Holland and Belgium were then called. The English general, John Churchill, who had been made Duke of Marlborough, led the armies of England and her allies to victory. As a result of this war Gibraltar at the southern tip of Spain and Nova Scotia in North America were added to the British Empire.

In 1707 England and Scotland at last became united under one Government, and the Scots sent members to sit in Parliament at Westminster.

Journeying from town to town was done by stage coach, which was often dangerous, as highwaymen lurked on the roads waiting to rob travellers. For short journeys about town sedan chairs were used.

HANOVERIAN ENGLAND

When Queen Anne died, leaving no children, the question was, who was to succeed her? The people were determined to have a Protestant ruler, and the Protestant nearest to the throne was George, Prince of Hanover, a great-grandson of James I. Accordingly he was invited to England and became King George I, although he could not speak a word of English.

Neither George I nor George II was much interested in English affairs, and the real governors of the country were the Cabinet, a small council of men chosen from both Houses of Parliament. Sir Robert Walpole, head of the Cabinet, was the first statesman to be called Prime Minister.

David Garrick was a famous actor alive at this time, Defoe wrote "Robinson Crusoe," and Smollett and Fielding were among the greatest of English novelists. Alexander Pope and Dr. Samuel Johnson were alive. Handel, a great musician who came from Germany, composed music which is still played today.

Artists like Reynolds and Gainsborough were painting pictures which can now be seen in the National Gallery, London.

Men like Chippendale and Sheraton were designing and making beautiful furniture, and people will still pay big prices for their chairs.

Houses were simple and beautiful and built mainly of red brick, with large windows. The brothers Adam designed many important buildings in London, Bath and other cities.

Again there was war with France, though the fighting was mostly in North America and India. England became the strongest nation on the seas. In India Robert Clive was fighting and winning more land for the East India Company, and the French army was turned out of India.

In 1759 Canada was taken from the French by James Wolfe, who cleverly captured Quebec on the St. Lawrence river, by climbing some very steep cliffs near the city and taking the French by surprise. Canada became another English colony.

In 1760 George III (nicknamed Farmer George) came to the throne. Farming improved. More care was given to the manuring of land and choosing the right crops to suit the soil. Fields were surrounded by hedges and stone walls. Farmers reared finer horses, sheep and cows, and butcher's meat improved in quality.

In 1775 trouble began in the American colonies. These disliked paying taxes to a king in a distant land. They rebelled, and under George Washington fought the English soldiers sent there to keep order. They defeated the English, and the thirteen colonies joined together and became a separate nation, the United States of America.

In 1788 the first English settlers arrived in eastern Australia, which had been discovered several years earlier by Captain Cook. New Zealand had been discovered at the same time.

James Watt showed how steam engines could be used to turn wheels. New machines were invented for spinning and weaving cloth.

Craftsmen who had always worked at home now had to go into factories to work these machines, which made goods more quickly and more cheaply than by hand. This we call the "Industrial Revolution". Life in the factories was miserable. They were badly built, dark and stuffy, and even little children had to work long hours for little pay.

Towns grew larger. Coal was used instead of wood, and the smoke from the factory chimneys blackened the whole countryside. Roads were improved and many canals were built.

In 1802 the first steamship, built by William Symington, steamed down the Clyde-Forth canal in Central Scotland, towing two laden boats.

In 1801 Ireland was joined to Great Britain and sent members to the English Parliament.

Until 1807 slaves were bought and sold to work in the colonies, but in this year such trade was forbidden. England was the first great country to take this step.

In the same year the London streets were first lit by gas.

Another war had begun with France because Napoleon wanted to make himself master of Europe. He was successful at first, but Admiral Lord Nelson won a big sea battle at Trafalgar, smashing the French navy, and

Napoleon was finally beaten on land by the Duke of Wellington at Waterloo in Belgium. Malta was taken from France, and the English have held it ever since. Napoleon was captured and imprisoned on St. Helena, a little island in the South Atlantic, where he died.

The English were proud of these victories, because they had stood alone against the whole of Europe. Trafalgar Square in London is named after the battle, and in it is a high monument to Nelson. There is also a bridge over the Thames called Waterloo Bridge. Though a new one has had to be built recently, it still keeps the old name.

Clothes were becoming more like those of modern times. Top hats and long trousers came into fashion, and women's dresses changed from wide to straighter skirts.

A great deal of smuggling went on round the coast to avoid the taxes on such things as tea, tobacco and rum.

Then began a time of improved machinery, increasing trade and prosperity, and of social reform, which means the improvement of the ways of living among people of all classes.

The first railway, built by George Stephenson, was opened in 1825 and ran between Stockton and Darlington in Yorkshire. The trains went as fast as 15 miles an hour, which many people thought very dangerous.

Roads were made harder and smoother. To collect money for their upkeep there were toll-gates where travellers had to pay before being allowed to pass through.

In 1829 Sir Robert Peel founded the London Police Force. They wore top hats and frock coats and were nicknamed "Peelers" or "Bobbies."

Until 1832 the new towns which had grown up round the factories were not able to send men to speak for them in Parliament. The Reform Acts changed this, though at first only those people who paid fairly big rents or who owned land were allowed to vote. It was not until 1884 that all men could vote.

New factory laws were passed in Parliament. These laws gradually lessened the long hours a day that men, women and children had been made to work, and very young children were no longer allowed to work in factories. The Government sent inspectors round the factories to see that these laws were carried out.

Michael Faraday invented the electric dynamo, which made it possible to send electric current over long distances. In course of time this power came into use for driving machinery in factories. The windmill, so much used for grinding the grain in country districts, gradually ceased to be used.

In 1833 all slaves were set free throughout the British Empire, and the Government paid the slave owners twenty million pounds to make good their losses.

VICTORIAN ENGLAND

In 1837 Victoria became Queen at the age of 18, and she reigned for 64 years. She married Albert, Prince of Saxe-Coburg and Gotha, who became Prince Consort — that is, the husband of a reigning queen.

At this time there were taxes on the wheat brought into the country from abroad, and therefore food cost a lot of money; poor people were obliged to go hungry. Sir Robert Peel at last removed these taxes, so that bread became cheaper. Taxes were taken off many other imported goods. Thus began the period of what is called "Free Trade".

In 1840 Sir Rowland Hill introduced the first stick-on postage stamp, the "Penny Black" so much sought after by collectors. Letters could go all over the country for one penny.

Sir James Simpson, a Scottish doctor, discovered the use of chloroform, so that painless operations could be performed.

The Crystal Palace was built in Hyde Park in 1851 to hold the Great Exhibition of Arts and Crafts. People came from all over the world to visit it. The next year it was moved to Sydenham Hill and there kept as an amusement park until it was destroyed by fire in 1936.

In the same year the first under-seas electric cable was laid from Dover to Calais, which meant that news from Europe could be telegraphed to London.

The Crimean War against Russia broke out in 1854, because England, Turkey and France feared that Russia was getting too powerful in the Eastern Mediterranean and might invade India. Russia was defeated.

During this war Florence Nightingale went to the front with trained nurses to look after the wounded. This was the first time there had been women nurses in war.

In 1857 the Indian Mutiny broke out, a rebellion by Indian soldiers against their English officers, because they were angry to see their lands taken from them by the East India Company. There were also religious difficulties. The Mutiny was put down and the Government of India came under the British crown. Queen Victoria sent a viceroy to Delhi.

England became the world's workshop. The coal, iron and steel, cotton and woollen trades grew larger and larger. English ships took goods all over the world.

Three attempts were made to lay a telegraph cable across the Atlantic, and it was finally achieved in 1868.

Horse trams appeared in London in 1861.

David Livingstone explored Central Africa and discovered Lake Tanganyika. Rhodesia, named after Cecil Rhodes, and other parts of Africa were added to the Empire.

Canada became a Dominion in 1867 and since then has had its own Government and managed its own affairs.

Great scientists of the time were Thomas Huxley and Charles Darwin. The latter wrote a book called "The Origin of Species," in which he put forward the theory that all life on the earth had evolved from simple forms, and that men and monkeys sprang from a common ancestor. This caused a stir through the country for many years.

In 1870 Parliament made it possible for all children to go to school, and some years later a law was passed saying that all children must attend school.

Gradually iron steamships took the place of wooden sailing ships in all the oceans of the world. England had more merchant ships than any other country.

Throughout the whole century there was trouble with the Irish, who wanted to govern themselves. Ireland did not get "Home Rule" until after many years of quarrelling and fighting.

Lewis Carroll, whose real name was Charles Dodgson, and who was a lecturer at Oxford University, wrote "Alice in Wonderland" and "Alice Through the Looking-Glass" and Robert Louis Stevenson wrote "Treasure Island."

Dr. Joseph Lister discovered the value of antiseptics, which kill germs in wounds, and help doctors to cure and prevent disease.

The first university college to be opened for women was Girton College at Cambridge in 1869. More and more girls were able to go to school.

Henry Irving and Ellen Terry were famous for their acting, mostly in the plays of Shakespeare at the Lyceum Theatre, London.

From about the middle of the century onwards, English people became very interested in games. Cricket was very popular, and the test matches with Australia were started. Large crowds went to watch football matches, and people who had gardens with lawns played croquet.

Bicycles appeared on the roads. At first they were called "penny farthings," because they had one big wheel like an English penny and one small wheel like a farthing. But the ordinary "safety" kind soon followed.

The Hansom cab was a favourite carriage when not more than two people wished to ride, and for larger parties the fly or "growler" was used.

The first electric train ran in London in 1890.

Bathing machines, sometimes pulled up and down the beach by horses as the tide came in and went out, were seen at all seaside places, and women wore large and thick bathing dresses down to their ankles.

People went to the music halls for amusement. Popular songs like "Daisy, Daisy" and "Ta-ra-ra-boom-de-ay" were sung there, and the comedian Dan Leno was the rage. The most famous music halls were the Empire and the Alhambra in Leicester Square, London.

In 1897 Queen Victoria celebrated her Diamond Jubilee, as she had reigned for sixty years. Everyone had a holiday and waved flags. All the streets were decorated and there was a long procession, with soldiers and sailors from all over the Empire.

Two years later the Boer War began. This was fought between the English and Dutch farmers, called Boers, in South Africa.

When gold was found in the Dutch Transvaal in South Africa, all sorts of people from Europe hurried there to dig for it, hoping to make their fortunes. These people upset the peaceful life of the Boers, and the Dutch government, under President Kruger, refused to grant them the rights of citizens. They were called 'uitlanders' or outsiders. Matters went from bad to worse, and at length war was declared.

At first things went against the British, for the Boers were crack shots and knew how to make use of cover in their own country. Fresh troops under Lord Roberts and Lord Kitchener were sent out from England and the Boers were at last overwhelmed. Thus the whole of South Africa became British, though the Dutch were given equal rights and sent members to the Parliament at Cape Town. The Union of South Africa was made a self-governing Dominion in 1910.

TWENTIETH CENTURY

Queen Victoria died in 1901, and Kings and Emperors came from all over the world to attend her funeral. Edward VII, her eldest son, became king.

Our own twentieth century had started. At first life in England seemed very settled for people with money. King Edward was fond of pleasure and London life was fashionable. Many people went to garden parties, horse races, the opera, theatres and enjoyed yachting.

Motoring was thought to be very fast at twenty miles an hour, and people rode in furs and goggles, while women wore veils to keep on their large hats.

German bands were familiar in almost every town. Standing at street corners, these German visitors played popular English tunes, German waltzes, and marches on their silver and brass instruments.

For cycling women wore baggy knickerbockers called "bloomers", but they never became very popular and soon disappeared.

All men who wished to be smart wore top hats and frock coats, while the commoner folk wore bowler hats.

Balloons were often seen floating across the sky, and at holiday times one of the amusements at the Crystal Palace was a balloon ascent.

It seemed to people in the early 1900's that life would always be like this, but things were happening which were to change it.

The first wireless message was sent from Cornwall to Newfoundland in 1902.

Keir Hardie started the Independent Labour Party. His idea was to improve the lives of workpeople, not only by giving them better wages, but by making them the owners of the factories, so that they would be working for themselves and not only for the benefit of their masters. This was "Socialism". Some Socialists became members of Parliament, Keir Hardie being one of them.

Trade Unions became more powerful. These were unions or societies of workers who agreed to act together for the common good. If they wanted higher wages or better conditions of work and the employers refused to grant them, the men would all stop work at the same time. That was called a "strike". Sometimes the masters refused to let the men work unless they agreed to their terms; that was called a "lock-out".

For various reasons, such as free education, better wages and shorter working hours, there became less difference between upper and lower classes, rich and poor. Ordinary men and women claimed the right to their say in the government of the country, and in the parks on Sundays all kinds of ideas were freely expressed, though some speakers got into trouble with the police.

Free libraries were opened where people could borrow books to read if they could not or did not want to buy them.

New universities were opened in different towns, and clever men who could not afford the fees could often go to them without paying.

The "moving picture" was a novelty, and there were early attempts at coloured films. These films were silent and not very good, and the music was played by pianists, sitting in front of the screen.

In 1908 men and women over 70 years of age who had not been able to save any money were given a small pension every week by the Government.

Many women wanted to vote for members of Parliament. As the Government would not grant them this right, they broke windows, chained themselves to railings, damaged famous works of art in picture galleries, and poured acid into letter boxes to call attention to themselves and force the Government to give them the "Vote." They were called Suffragettes, and their leader was Mrs. Pankhurst. Many of them went to prison.

Major-General – afterwards Lord – Baden-Powell, who had been one of the popular heroes of the Boer War, founded the Boy Scout movement in 1908 and became Chief Scout. He also founded the Girl Guides.

In the same year Bleriot, a Frenchman, flew from near Calais to Dover in an aeroplane.

Clothes became cheaper and could be bought ready made in shops. The result was that people looked better dressed, and the raggedness which had been noticeable in Victorian days was less seen.

Women's fashions changed almost from year to year. A very strange one was the "hobble skirt," but generally clothes were getting more comfortable and in keeping with the times.

In 1911 Mr. Lloyd George passed the National Insurance Act through Parliament. Each week workers and masters paid money to the Government so that if a man were ill or out of work part of his wages would be paid to him during that time. It was a step forward towards removing the fear of unemployment, and was one of the first important reforms in the reign of George V, who had become king one year before.

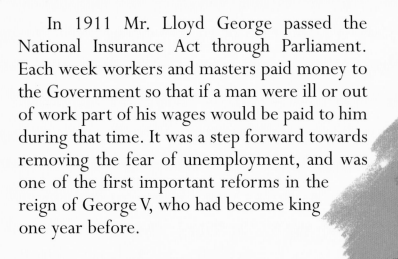

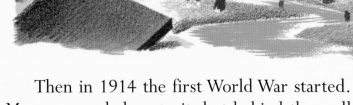

Then in 1914 the first World War started. Many causes led up to it, but behind them all was the ambition of Germany, led by the Kaiser William II, to be the master of Europe. Austria and some of the Balkan countries fought on the German side.

England, France, Russia, Italy, America, Japan and Serbia combined to fight against them. It was the biggest war ever known. The armies on both sides ran into millions of men, and for the first time in England men were conscripted – that is they had by law to join the army, even if they did not want to.

Tanks were used for fighting for the first time, and so were aeroplanes. These carried small guns with which to fire at each other, and England had its first air raids from lighter-than-air machines. These airships were long cigar-shaped balloons driven by propellers and called Zeppelins, after the German Count Zeppelin who invented them. It was soon found that they were easy to shoot down, and the small but faster aeroplane was more successful.

The Royal Navy patrolled the seas, and protected the merchant ships, which were bringing food and munitions to England, against the German submarines.

After four years of terrible fighting, in which millions of soldiers were killed on both sides, the Germans, who had almost won the war in the first few months, were at last defeated. The order to cease fire came suddenly at 11 o'clock on the 11th November, 1918. This was called Armistice Day. Everyone was happy because the war was over.

Nov. 11th 1918

After this war many changes came into the lives of the English people. Women had taken a great part in the war, as bus conductors, army lorry drivers, nurses, munition workers, and had helped to keep the ordinary business of the country going, and quite rightly they were given the Vote, so that they could help to choose the members of Parliament.

MUNITION WORKER

BUS CONDUCTOR

FARM WORKER

BELFAST

IRELAND

DUBLIN

In 1921 Ireland was divided into two. The Northern counties called Ulster, with Belfast as its capital, remained part of Great Britain; while the South, around Dublin, was given Home Rule and became the Irish Free State, with its own Parliament.

After the war there was much new building. All along the main roads leading out of London and the big towns, miles of small houses were built and much beautiful country was spoilt. Proper planning could have stopped this but it seemed nobody's business to plan. Some good attempts were made to replace the inconvenient and dirty old houses in the towns with modern blocks of flats and "garden cities", but it did not seem possible to do enough.

In some towns new buildings made of concrete and even of steel and glass were put up, which were light, simple and clean looking.

A Scotsman, John Baird, made the first experiments in television, and some people were able to watch a horse race, perhaps, as they sat in an armchair at home.

"Talkies" took the place of silent pictures, and many more people began to go to the cinema.

In 1919 two Englishmen flew across the Atlantic Ocean for the first time from Newfoundland to Ireland.

More and more air services appeared. Business men flew between London, Manchester, Birmingham and other big towns – as well as to and from the Continent of Europe.

The London and North Eastern Railway built the Flying Scotsman, the fastest engine in the world at the time.

"London Transport" improved the Underground Railways in speed, distance and comfort. Many new stations were built and old ones were altered and decorated with gay posters, often designed by famous artists.

Motor cars were produced in such large numbers that they could be sold cheaply. Many more people owned their own cars.

With the larger number of cars on the roads, however, there came traffic problems.

There were so many accidents and hold-ups at cross roads that Mr. Hore Belisha arranged a set of rules for all users of roads. All over the country new traffic lights and "Belisha beacons" were put up, which did reduce the number of accidents and made travelling easier.

As in every other country, the general speed of travel increased. Everything became streamlined.

The Labour Party was becoming more important in the government of the country, and in 1924 for the first time, with Ramsay MacDonald as Prime Minister, a Labour Government was formed. It did not last long.

In the late twenties there was a boom in trade, and many business people made large fortunes.

Then in 1929 everything "slumped," and many big factories had to close down because they had no work to do, as few people could afford to buy their goods. The number of men and women who were unemployed increased enormously, and the Government had to pay out millions of pounds a year to the unemployed to keep them from starving.

This money was called the "dole," but in spite of it many could not get enough food.

At the same time improvements were being made in living conditions. People went hiking, and cheap railway tickets brought the country nearer to those who lived in the cities. The British Broadcasting Corporation provided entertainment for the home. More people played outdoor games, and B.B.C. broadcasts of cricket, tennis, football and boxing matches became increasingly popular.

There were refrigerators to keep food fresh and cool, and electric vacuum cleaners to make housework easier. Women wore shorter skirts and cut their hair short too, and found themselves more free to work in offices if they wished.

In 1935 George V and Queen Mary celebrated their twenty-fifth year on the throne. It was called the Silver Jubilee. There were parties, fireworks, floodlighting and processions for a whole week. The weather was sunny, and London was crowded with visitors who wanted to catch a glimpse of the King and Queen. In the evenings bands came out on to the balconies of hotels and people danced in the streets.

Shortly after this George V died, and the Prince of Wales came to the throne as Edward VIII, but he was never crowned as he did not wish to be king. He took the title of Duke of Windsor and left England. His brother was crowned George VI in 1937.

Although everything seemed to be going so well, most people felt that it would not last, and that trouble was coming again. They were right.

Under its new leader, Adolf Hitler, Germany was again threatening to conquer first Europe and later the whole world, with the help of Italy and Japan. Germany and Italy were "Fascist" states. They did not believe in democracy and government by Parliament. They said there should be only one voice in the country, the Leader's voice. Hitler intended to be the Leader of the world.

There were some Fascists in England, too. They wore uniforms and were called Blackshirts. If the Fascists disliked anything, they believed they must clear it away by force, and there were many street fights in the bigger towns, especially in the East End of London, a neighbourhood in which lived great numbers of Jewish people, for whom the Fascists had a special hate.

In September 1939 Hitler's armies attacked Poland, which Great Britain and France had promised to help, so these two countries declared war on Germany on September 3rd, and the second great World War had begun.

Very soon the Dominions (now called the British Commonwealth of Nations) joined in too.

In Great Britain all the windows had to be blacked out at night and no lights could be shown in the streets, so that German aeroplanes could not see where to drop their bombs. At night people had to find their way about the streets with flash lamps.

For a time there was not much fighting on land, but German submarines tried to stop ships carrying food and munitions from reaching England. Both men and women joined the Navy, Army and R.A.F. Others learnt what they should do if there were air raids. This was called Civil Defence.

Then in the spring of 1940 Germany first attacked Norway and then overran Holland, Belgium and France. Winston Churchill became the British Prime Minister. Very soon the Germans took Paris and the French Government was forced to ask for an armistice. Great Britain and the Empire stood alone against Germany and Italy – which at this time entered the war.

Many kinds of food were rationed so that everyone should get a fair share. Later on clothes were also rationed.

Then came the Battle of Britain, in which masses of German aeroplanes attacked the British Isles in day time; but the British pilots destroyed many and drove the others back. Later came the night raids when London and many other cities were bombed. People spent their nights in air raid shelters underground, while firemen fought the flames and wardens helped the injured. But the spirit of the people did not fail, and gradually the attacks weakened.

In 1941 Mr. Churchill and President Roosevelt drew up the "Atlantic Charter", which sets forth the war aims of the freedom-loving peoples and their plans for the future peace.

In the summer of 1941 Germany attacked the Soviet Union, so that Russia and Britain became allies. At first the Germans were victorious and the Russians had to retreat until they were not far from their capital, Moscow. But after the battle of Stalingrad the tide turned, and step by step the Germans were driven back. Britain and America supplied Russia with great quantities of guns, tanks and aeroplanes.

On December 7th, 1941, Japan made a surprise attack on Pearl Harbour, on one of the Hawaiian islands in the Pacific Ocean belonging to the United States of America. After this America joined with Great Britain, Russia and China and many other countries, now called the "United Nations". Germany, Italy, Japan and the countries fighting with them were called the "Axis".

The United Nations suffered many severe blows in the Far East and in North Africa, largely because they did not have enough aeroplanes and modern weapons of war. But gradually they became stronger and stronger, and Germany was bombed from the air as Britain had been earlier. The Germans were driven out of North Africa and the Italian Government surrendered in September 1943.

The leaders of the four great powers, Churchill, Roosevelt, Stalin and Chiang Kaishek, agreed to fight together to rid the world of Fascism and to be friends after victory.

England became a military camp, a stepping stone for the invasion of Hitler's Europe. Troops of all nationalities trained side by side, refugees from the conquered countries, millions of American soldiers and airmen, and a great British and Commonwealth Army. Factories in Britain and America turned out streams of goods which the Navy convoyed to all parts of the World.

Then, when everyone had learned to work together, the attack was launched. The Anglo-American Armies under General Eisenhower and General Montgomery landed in Northern France on June 6th, 1944. In a year this army made its way to Berlin, there meeting the Russians who had all the time been advancing from the East. On May 8th 1945, war with Germany ended. The Germans had already ceased fighting in Italy, and Japan was left alone, to be defeated on August 15th of the same year.

A year later the end of this disastrous war was celebrated by the Victory Parade, when men and women of all the services and all countries, and their civilian helpers, passed through London in a big procession. There were firework displays all over the country.

This brings us to the end of our history, and the hopes of men and women all over the world that the folly of war, and the dreadful misery it brings, may at last be understood, and never repeated. That such a Peace shall be made that, as the Atlantic Charter declares: 'All men in all lands may live out their lives in freedom from fear and want'.